SPACE FIRSTS™

DENNIS TITO
The First Space Tourist

Heather Feldman

The Rosen Publishing Group's
PowerKids Press™
New York

For my loving sister and brother, Lauren Hochman and Jonathan Lowenberg, for helping to light my path with stars

Published in 2003 by The Rosen Publishing Group, Inc.
29 East 21st Street, New York, NY 10010

First Edition

Editor: Nancy MacDonell Smith
Book Design: Mike Donnellan

Photo Credits: Cover, pp. 12, 20 © Reuters NewMedia Inc./CORBIS; p. 4 © Frederick M. Brown/Getty Images; p. 7 © Laski Diffusion/Getty Images; pp. 8, 16 (top right), 19 © Getty Images; pp. 11, 15 © AFP/CORBIS; p. 16 © Oleg Nakihshin/Getty Images.

Feldman, Heather.
Dennis Tito, the first space tourist / Heather Feldman.— 1st ed.
      p. cm. — (Space firsts)
Includes bibliographical references and index.
Summary: Details the journey of Dennis Tito, the wealthy businessman who made a trip into space by purchasing a seat aboard a Russian spacecraft.
ISBN 0-8239-6249-0 (library binding)
1. Tito, Dennis, 1940– —Juvenile literature. 2. Aerospace engineers—United States—Biography—Juvenile literature. 3. Space tourism—Juvenile literature. 4. Tourists—United States—Biography—Juvenile literature. 5. Businesspeople—United States—Biography—Juvenile literature. [1. Tito, Dennis, 1940– 2. Space flight.] I. Title.
TL540.T556 F44 2003
910'.919'092—dc21

                              2001007784

Manufactured in the United States of America

Contents

Who Is Dennis Tito?

Dennis Tito is the first person to have visited space as a **tourist**. Since he was a young boy, Tito had dreamed of traveling to space. He made his dream a reality by purchasing a seat aboard a Russian **space shuttle** and traveling to space with a team of Russian **cosmonauts**.

Dennis Tito grew up in Queens, New York. His mother was a seamstress, and his father was a printer. As a young man, Tito was fascinated by space. He always remembered the first **satellite** he saw in the sky, in 1961. Tito went on to study **aerospace engineering**. In 1964, he got a job at a laboratory in Pasadena, California, to design flight paths for the National Aeronautics and Space Administration (NASA).

When Dennis Tito finally realized his lifelong goal, he described himself as, "One happy guy, one happy man—very happy!"

A New Career

Dennis Tito enjoyed working as a space engineer, but he was not earning enough money to support his family. He had a lot of bills to pay. Tito began **investing** money in the stock market. After several years, Tito and his wife, Suzanne, started their own business, called Wilshire Associates. The Titos were very successful and soon became millionaires. Tito built one of the largest houses in Los Angeles, California, which he often referred to as his "own little space station." Tito was no longer a space engineer, but he was now wealthy enough to make his lifelong dream a reality. He began to take steps to make that dream come true.

Dennis Tito paid $20 million for his trip to space. This was enough money to pay all the costs for the mission.

Space Adventures

In 1991, Dennis Tito took a trip to Moscow, Russia. It was during this trip that Tito first thought about taking a space vacation. Several years later, Tito went to a company called Space Adventures for help. Space Adventures is a space tourist company. Its goal is to make space vacations a reality. Space Adventures helped Tito book a seat on a Russian space shuttle.

Tito was Space Adventures' first client to journey into space. Space Adventures helped Tito plan his trip, and with the aid of several Russian space agencies, provided him with the proper training. "Space Adventures has prepared me for the **ultimate** exploration experience, a flight into space," said Tito. "It is really a **privilege** to be involved in the first **mission** of this kind and to lead the way for other private citizens to do the same thing."

Dennis Tito blasted into space on a Russian Soyuz spacecraft. The Soyuz spacecraft is used to bring cosmonauts to and from space.

Preparing for Flight

Tito worked hard to prepare for his flight into space. He lived in Russia for eight months, where he spent 900 hours in cosmonaut training. He studied and passed all of his tests. The crew's flight engineer, Yuri Baturin, told him, "We are very happy to accompany you to space."

Dennis Tito took his role aboard the Russian spacecraft very seriously. He said, "This is not a vacation, it's a fulfillment of a life's dream to fly to space." For Tito, becoming the 415th person to fly into space was a privilege and an honor. In his words, this journey would be "the ultimate human adventure."

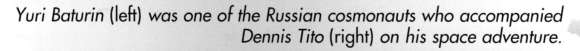

Yuri Baturin (left) *was one of the Russian cosmonauts who accompanied Dennis Tito* (right) *on his space adventure.*

NASA Disapproves

When Dennis Tito arrived to finish the last part of his training at the Johnson Space Center in Houston, Texas, NASA officials objected. Not everyone shared Tito's excitement about his trip to space. NASA felt that Tito had not received enough training to travel to space. Officials from Japan, Canada, and many European countries were also opposed to Tito's adventure. These officials believed that Tito was a safety risk and that his presence onboard the spacecraft could cause problems for the crew.

NASA eventually agreed to let Tito complete his training. However, NASA insisted that Tito sign an agreement that held him responsible for his own safety. NASA did not want to be responsible if something went wrong and Tito was injured.

NASA chief Daniel Goldin was one of the people who objected to Dennis Tito's plan to become the first space tourist. In the end, NASA agreed to let Tito make the trip.

13

The Big Day

On April 28, 2001, Dennis Tito boarded the Russian *Soyuz* spacecraft with his crewmates, Yuri Baturin and Talgat Musabayev. Dennis Tito was 60 years old, and his lifelong dream was about to begin. The crew was headed to the **International Space Station** *(ISS)*, a space station shared by 16 countries. The trip would last for eight days.

The spacecraft **launched** from the Baikonur Cosmodrome in Kazakhstan, in central Asia. Tito experienced some motion sickness at first, but he felt better quickly and was able to enjoy his wonderful journey. Tito was in space!

A happy Dennis Tito (left) *shakes hands with his crew members, Talgat Musabayev* (center) *and Yuri Baturin* (right). *Musabayev said having Tito onboard was "no problem at all."*

Dennis Tito in Space

Dennis Tito was thrilled to be in space. The flight to the space station went well. There were a few minor problems, but nothing serious. Tito spent two days in the Russian spacecraft and six days on the *ISS*. While on the *ISS*, he took many photographs and videos, listened to opera music, and assisted the crew with light duties. One of Tito's favorite parts of the trip was looking out his window and seeing Earth! He said being in space "goes well beyond anything that I have ever dreamed. Living in space is like having a different life, living in a different world." He loved it so much, he said, "I could have stayed up there for months."

Dennis Tito said, "Khorosho," to the TV audience watching his journey. Khorosho *means "good" in Russian.* Inset: *Tito relaxes in his seat on the* ISS.

Return to Earth

The trip from the space station back to Earth took three hours. The spacecraft bounced a lot as it reentered Earth's **atmosphere**, but no one was hurt. On May 6, 2001, Dennis Tito landed safely back on Earth. The spacecraft touched down in Kazakhstan. Tito was tired but thrilled with his experience. "It was **paradise**," he said, "I just came back from paradise." He was a little pale and had some trouble walking at first. He was so happy, though, that those things didn't seem to matter to him. After the spacecraft landed, Tito and his crewmates were flown to a military airport outside of Moscow. A military band and many anxious reporters greeted the cosmonauts and their space tourist. Everyone wanted to hear about Tito's adventure in space.

After fulfilling his dream, Dennis Tito was tired but extremely happy. He was sick to his stomach only once during his eight-day trip.

Dennis Tito Speaks Out

Upon his return from space, Dennis Tito began speaking out about space tourism. Tito has been giving speeches and talking to reporters. Even though NASA had been against his trip to space, Tito has suggested that NASA set aside one seat on each flight of the space shuttle for a tourist. He believes that poets, musicians, and teachers should all go to space. He said, "We've been in space for 40 years, and we don't have it in our music or literature or poetry." Tito believes that if poets and artists go to space, they will be able to describe what it's like there for everyone else. Tito feels strongly that he has cleared the way for future space tourists. He feels that ordinary citizens and not just wealthy individuals should be able to fly to space. He hopes that one day soon, other people can take a trip to space, as he did.

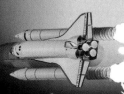

Dennis Tito has become an outspoken supporter of space tourism. Tito has no plans to return to space himself. "I am ready to get back to my normal life," he said.

21

Space Tourism

Dennis Tito is not the only person who thinks there should be tourists in space. There are already several space-tourism companies that are planning to build **suborbital** vehicles, **orbital** hotels, and even **lunar** cruise ships within the next 20 years! These companies have invested millions of dollars in the hope that the space tourism industry will take off. It is becoming clear that selling tickets to fly to space could become a very **lucrative** business. It is possible that sometime in the future, people may not only be going to the beach for vacation, but also to space.

Glossary

aerospace engineering (EHR-oh-spays en-jih-NEER-ing) The profession of scientists who study the atmosphere and the space beyond as a whole.

atmosphere (AT-muh-sfeer) The layer of gases that surrounds an object in space. On Earth, this layer is air.

cosmonauts (KOZ-muh-nahts) The Russian word for astronauts.

International Space Station (in-ter-NASH-nul SPAYS STAY-shun) The largest and most complex scientific project in history. Sixteen countries around the world work together to run the space station. Also called the *ISS*.

investing (in-VEST-ing) Putting money into something, such as a company, in the hope of getting more money later on.

launched (LAWNCHD) Pushed into the air.

lucrative (LOO-kruh-tiv) Bringing in money or profit.

lunar (LOO-ner) Of or about the Moon.

mission (MIH-shun) A special job or task.

orbital (OR-bih-tul) Of or about the circular path traveled by a satellite or a spacecraft.

paradise (PAR-uh-dys) A wonderful place or a state of happiness.

privilege (PRIHV-lij) A special right or favor.

satellite (SA-til-yt) A human-made or natural object that orbits another body.

space shuttle (SPAYS SHUH-tul) A reusable spacecraft designed to travel to and from space carrying people and cargo.

suborbital (sub-OR-bih-tul) Falling short of a complete orbit.

tourist (TUR-ist) Any person who takes a trip or a tour for pleasure.

ultimate (UL-tuh-mit) The highest or best possible.

Index

Web Sites

Due to the changing nature of Internet links, PowerKids Press has developed an online list of Web sites related to the subject of this book. This site is updated regularly. Please use this link to access the list:
www.powerkidslinks.com/sf/dentito/